W9-BLR-519

R03017 16720

CHICAGO PUBLIC LIBRARY
ORIOLE PARK

R0035733963

DISCARD

DATE DUE

DEMCO 38-296

ORIOLE PARK BRANCH
7454 W. BALMORAL AVE.
CHICAGO, IL. 60656

© THE BAKER & TAYLOR CO.

Halloween Fun

Messner Holiday Library
Halloween Fun
by Judith Hoffman Corwin

Julian Messner New York

Copyright © 1983 Judith Hoffman Corwin

All rights reserved including the right of
reproduction in whole or in part in any form.

Published by Julian Messner,
a division of Simon & Schuster, Inc.
Simon & Schuster Building,
1230 Avenue of the Americas,
New York, New York 10020.

Manufactured in the United States of America

Design by Judith Hoffman Corwin
10 9 8 7 6 5 4 3 2
10 9 8 7 6 5 4 3 2 1 Pbk.
Library of Congress Cataloging in Publication Data

Corwin, Judith Hoffman.
  Halloween fun.

  (Messner holiday library)
  Includes index.
  Summary: Describes Halloween customs and gives
directions for making Halloween costumes, greeting
cards, decorations, presents, and things to eat, using
materials that are usually found around the house.
    1. Halloween decorations—Juvenile literature.
2. Holiday cookery—Juvenile literature. [1. Halloween. 2. Halloween decorations. 3. Cookery.
4. Holidays] I. Title. II. Series.
TT900.H32C67 1983   745.594′1   83-8289
ISBN 0-671-49421-X
ISBN 0-671-49756-1 Pbk.

R03017 16720

For Oliver Jamie
my very own "trick or treater"

MESSNER BOOKS BY JUDITH HOFFMAN CORWIN

The Messner Holiday Library: Halloween Fun

The Messner Holiday Library: Christmas Fun

The Messner Holiday Library: Valentine Fun

Contents

For You

Halloween is the time for parties and fun, and for pumpkins carved into jack-o'-lanterns to put by the window to light your way back from your adventures.

On Halloween, it's great fun to dress up—perhaps as a monster, a witch, a ghost, or something else very special and go with friends from door to door for candy and other goodies. It's also fun to look at all your treats when you get home and to decide what to eat now and what to save. You may find you have collected enough to last you until Thanksgiving! But before you eat any of your treats, make sure they are safe, that they are properly wrapped and do not have anything in them that should not be eaten.

HALLOWEEN FUN will help you to enjoy Halloween in many ways: making costumes, greeting cards, decorations, presents, and good things to eat. You will be able to make everything yourself, using mostly things that you can find around the house. You will also learn why we do some of the things we do on Halloween.

About Halloween

The people who lived in Scotland and Ireland in ancient times were called the Celts. The Celts held a special festival to honor Samhain, the god of the dead, on what was their New Year's Eve—October 31 by our calendar. Huge bonfires were set to scare away any evil spirits that might harm the people or the herds of cattle and sheep returning from the pastures where they had grazed all summer. The souls of the dead were thought to revisit their homes during this time.

This Celtic festival was turned into another celebration during the Middle Ages in Scotland and Ireland. All Hallows—a feast in honor of all the Christian saints—was celebrated on November 1. But on All Hallows' Eve people believed that witches, sometimes in the form of black cats, flew about and ghosts, demons, and goblins were thought to roam the land. All Hallows' Eve was also supposed to be the time to tell the future—who would marry whom, how long they would live, and if they would be lucky. It was also a time for games like bobbing for apples that we play to this day. The Irish believed that "the little people" played pranks on Halloween, and so mischief-making became part of the festivities. "All Hallows' Eve" became "Halloween," and about 150 years ago the Scots and Irish carried the Halloween tradition to America.

A favorite symbol of Halloween is the jack-o'-lantern. The name "jack-o'-lantern" may have come from some night watchman who carried a lantern on his rounds. A hollowed-out turnip was used in Scotland but the pumpkin is native to the United States and is used here. A new Halloween tradition is growing in the United States, where children are going trick-or-treating to collect money for UNICEF, the United Nations International Children's Emergency Fund. Every Halloween, millions of children in the United States help others around the world who are less fortunate than they are.

Before You Begin

Make your own pattern

Directions for most of the projects in this book include patterns for you to make an exact copy of what is shown. You don't want to cut up the book, so make your own patterns with tracing paper. Begin by placing a piece of tracing paper over the pattern to be transferred from the book. Using a pencil with soft lead, trace over the outline of what is in the book. When you have finished, cut out what you have drawn on the tracing paper. Now you have your own pattern.

Using your pattern

Pin your pattern, tape it or hold it down carefully on the paper or fabric you have chosen to work with. Draw around the edges of the pattern. Then lift up the tracing paper pattern and go on with the other instructions for your project.

Materials you will need

The basic materials you need are readily available from stationery stores and art supply shops: cardboard, oaktag, heavy white paper, and colored paper. Extras like cloth and bits of lace may be found at home or at fabric departments in stores. For details or accents you'll need colored markers (waterproof), pencils, or watercolors. You will also need a sharp pair of scissors and a good brand of white glue.

Preparing a work area

Before starting to work, make sure that all your supplies are at hand and that everything is neat and clean. Cover your work surface with newspaper to protect it from glue. By the way, when you work with glue always spread a thin, even coat. A thin coat sticks better and is less likely to cause the paper to buckle.

For the cooking projects you will need an adult to help you with the stove.

Most projects in **Halloween Fun** can be made quite easily. Some may prove more of a challenge—but you can do them all. Have fun!

A Word About Costumes

Part of the fun on Halloween is dressing up. You can create your own costumes. Almost anything goes on Halloween night. Experiment with things that you find around the house. Use your imagination when you are hunting for the perfect costume.

To help you, here are some ideas for some super-quick costumes that you can make—a ghost, a witch, Count and Countess Morbida, and Robert Robot for a more modern approach! There are also instructions for masks, Dracula's blood, some ghostly white makeup, scars, white plastic vampire's teeth, and a horror hand. Feel free to "mix and match" these things to create your own masters and mistresses of mischief!

Super Cape

This cape is so simple to make and has many uses for Halloween.

MATERIALS:

1 square yard of black felt. (You can also use
   any solid color felt or other fabric, or an old
   sheet.)
2 pieces of black ribbon, 12″ long
needle, black thread
scissors
light-colored crayon or chalk.

METHOD:

1. ☆ Draw the outline of the cape on the fabric, using the illustration as a guide.

2. ☆ Cut along the lines that you have drawn on the felt.

3. ☆ At each side of one end (see illustration) sew a piece of ribbon in place so that you can tie the finished cape around you.

I really put
my
into
it!

Batty T-Shirt

This black bat will fly onto your T-shirt and stay forever. You can also have fun with two other designs: the superstar T-shirt and "I really put my foot in it."

MATERIALS:

white T-shirt
tracing paper
carbon paper
pencil, tape
cardboard
black and red felt tip markers

METHOD:

1. ☆ Trace the bat design, using tracing paper.

2. ☆ Lay the T-shirt on the work surface so that the shirt is perfectly flat. Front should face you. Slip a piece of cardboard into the shirt. This will prevent the marker ink from going onto the back of the shirt.

3. ☆ Place a piece of carbon paper on top of the T-shirt and tape it down. Now tape the traced bat design on top of the carbon paper. Check the illustration for placement.

4. ☆ Draw over the design firmly with a pencil. Then remove the tracing and carbon paper from the T-shirt, leaving the cardboard in place. Now draw over the design with a black felt tip marker.

5. ☆ Color in the eyes red and the rest of the bat black.

For the **superstar T-shirt**, start by putting the cardboard inside the T-shirt. Draw a star with the red marker and write "SUPER" in black.

Use the same procedure as above for the "**I really put my foot into it**" shirt. Put the cardboard in the shirt and then write the message with a black marker. Then put your foot on the shirt and draw its outline. Color it.

13

Ghastly Ghost

Ghosts are a favorite at Halloween. Here's one to make from an old sheet in a flash!

MATERIALS:

old white sheet
scissors
pencil
black felt tip marker

METHOD:

1. ☆ Before beginning this project look at the illustration.

2. ☆ Place the sheet over your head and check that it covers your clothes completely.

3. ☆ As you take the sheet off, grasp the part of it which covered your head. Draw the face on this part with a pencil, checking the illustration.

4. ☆ Now go over the pencil lines with a black marker.

5. ☆ Cut out the two circles for eyes, but leave the marker outlines for a more scary effect. Make sure that the holes are large enough for you to see through.

6. ☆ If you wish you can also cut out two holes to put your hands through (so you can reach out and get the goodies!). To do this put the sheet on again and feel where your hands would be comfortable coming through. Mark these spots with a pencil, then take the sheet off, and cut an opening about 4″ square at each of the marked spots.

Count and Countess Morbida

Most monsters have a ghostly pale complexion and here's how to make yourself look that way. The Count and his Countess both wear this special makeup with the cape and Batty T-shirt.

MATERIALS:

cornstarch
cold cream or hand lotion
cotton balls
black eyebrow pencil
brown, grey or purple eye shadow
red lipstick

METHOD:

1. ☆ First spread a thin layer of cold cream or hand lotion all over your face. Then with a cotton ball pat on some cornstarch.

2. ☆ If you have permission to use someone's makeup, draw outlines around your eyes and mouth with a dark eyebrow pencil. Then put some eye shadow on and finish with some bright red lipstick.

Wanda Witch

Wanda Witch wears ghostly white makeup. Outline your eyes with a black eyebrow pencil and put some dark eye shadow on your eyelids. Red lipstick is great fun too! Wanda Witch can wear a cape of black felt and a Batty T-shirt if you like.

MATERIALS:

black oaktag (hat)
white paper (nose)
straight pin, scissors
thread, stapler

METHOD:

1. ☆ To make the witch's hat make a cone from the cardboard. Try it on to see that it will fit and then staple the ends closed.

2. ☆ To make the witch's nose repeat what you did for the hat, only use the white paper and make the cone much smaller (so that it will fit over your nose). Make tiny holes at the base with a pin, one on each side. Attach the thread to the holes. Now your witch's nose will stay on!

3. ☆ For the brim of the hat cut a circle from the oaktag (as shown) and cut out the inside so that it fits over the cone of the hat.

Robert Robot

This little guy will prove that Halloween is definitely not old-fashioned!

MATERIALS:

cardboard box large enough to fit over your
  body and reach to your knees or waist
cardboard box large enough to fit over your
  head
cereal box
tinfoil
two paper cups
black oaktag
two corks
metal coat hanger
egg carton
twelve bottle caps or metal washers
silver paint (optional)
scissors, pencil, ruler, tape, glue, paintbrush
  (optional)

METHOD:

1. ☆ For the robot's body: Take the largest box and cut the lid and flaps off one end. With the open end down, hold the box so that the top of it is even with your shoulders. Have someone mark the places on the sides of the box where your arms will come through. Cut out armholes about 7″ square. Now cut a hole at the center of the unopened end of the box big enough for your head to pass through.

2. ☆ For the robot's head: Cut the lid and flaps off one end of the second box. With the open end down, rest the box on one shoulder and hold it next to your head. Now have

someone mark a line even with your eyes. Cut an opening, as shown, 7" across and 2" high, centered along the line just marked. This opening is the first step in making eyes for the robot.

3. ☆ Complete the robot's eyes by cutting two circles, each 5" in diameter, from tinfoil. Center the circles on the eye openings in the box, as shown. Glue down. Pierce and fold in along the opening in the box. Cover eight bottle caps with tinfoil. Glue four around each eye of the robot, as shown. Metal washers can be used in place of the foil-covered bottle caps.

4. ☆ To make the robot's mouth: Cut a piece of black oaktag 3" square and glue it below the robot's eyes, as shown. Find the center of the square of oaktag and mark with a pencil. From this center mark draw a circle $1\frac{1}{2}$" in diameter. Now cut out around the circle, leaving the opening for the mouth.

5. ☆ For the robot's ears: Cover two paper cups with tinfoil, then glue one to each side of the head.

6. ☆ Antennae for the robot are made with two pieces of wire from a coat hanger, each about 12" long. Place a cork at one end of each piece of wire. Stick the other end of each wire piece through the top of the robot's head. Check the illustration for placement. Bend the uncovered wire ends to fit along the inside top of the box. Cover with masking tape so there will be no sharp points.

7. ☆ Complete the robot's head by cutting a circle of black oaktag, 3" in diameter. Cut this circle in half. Now take either half (throw

away the other or share it with someone), and glue it above the eyes, as shown.

8. ☆ Controls for the robot are placed on the body box. To make the controls, first wrap a cereal box in tinfoil. This box should be glued to the body box about 5" down from the center. Next, take the bottom portion of an egg carton and cut it in half. With markers of different colors, color in each of the sections in the carton bottom. Now glue the carton bottom to the cereal box, as shown.

Make four knobs by covering bottle caps with tinfoil as in Step 3. Place on body box below control box, as shown.

9. ☆ Robot's head can be glued or taped to its body or the head and body can be worn as two separate pieces.

Optional: Robot's head and body can be painted with silver paint; this should be done before the robot's face is made.

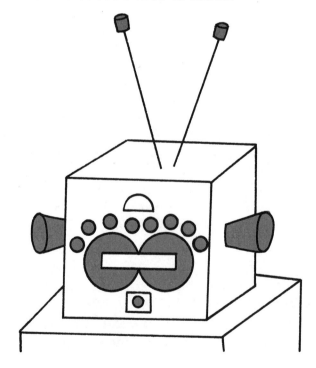

Horror Hands

These monster Horror Hands can either be worn as part of your Halloween costume or left ghoulishly around the house.

MATERIALS:

loose fitting rubber gloves
strips of gauze bandage
black felt tip marker
talcum powder
red paint
glue
newspaper

METHOD:

1. ☆ First stuff the glove with newspaper. This will make it easier for you to work with it.

2. ☆ With the felt tip marker go over the fingernails to make them look ghoulish.

3. ☆ Beginning with the fingers, wrap gauze strips around the entire glove until it is completely bandaged. Glue the gauze down as you are working to keep it from unraveling.

4. ☆ You can make one hand and wear it, keeping the other hand hidden under your costume—or make two hands if you like.

5. ☆ For a final horrible touch sprinkle red paint on your Horror Hands until they are nice and "bloody." Before you wear your Horror Hands sprinkle talcum powder into the inside of the gloves so that they won't stick to your hands. (Don't forget to remove the newspaper first!)

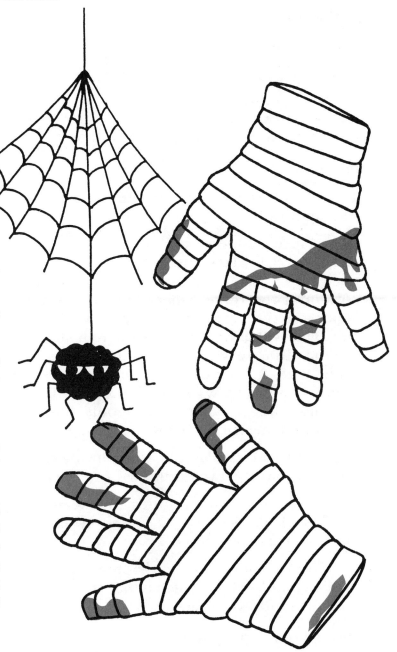

Fierce Monster Mask

This scary mask would go well with the cape.

MATERIALS:

white oaktag
tracing paper
carbon paper
pencil, scissors
string, straight pin
felt tip markers in red and black, tape

METHOD:

1. ☆ Trace the design for the mask with tracing paper.

2. ☆ Place a sheet of carbon paper over the white oaktag. Place the traced design over the carbon paper. Gently tape the top and bottom of the three papers (oaktag, carbon paper, and tracing paper) onto your work surface. This will prevent the papers from sliding around. Draw over the lines of the design again with a pencil, making sure to press evenly and firmly. When you lift off the tracing and carbon papers you should have a copy of the design on the white oaktag.

3. ☆ Cut out the mask from the oaktag. Then cut out the two circles for the eyes.

4. ☆ Draw over all the lines on the mask with black marker. Color in the eyebrows black and the mouth red.

5. ☆ Make a hole on each side of the ears with a pin. Attach a string so that you can tie the mask onto your face.

Now go out and scare somebody!

20

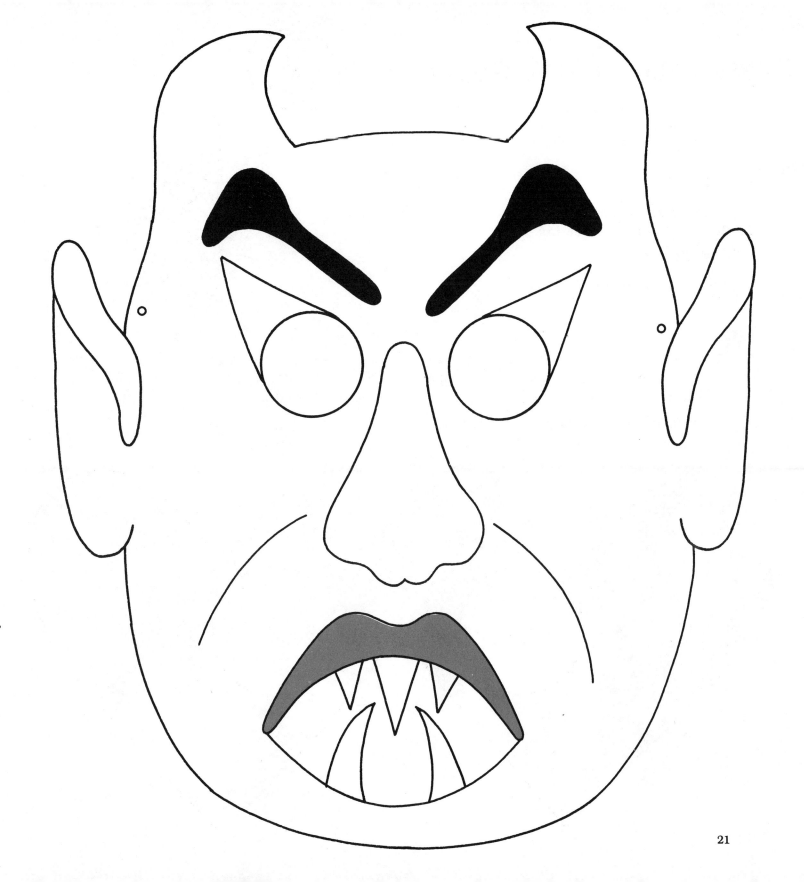

21

Black Mask, or Red-Heart Mask

These go nicely with almost any costume.

MATERIALS:

1 square black or red felt
black or red ribbon or string
tracing paper
pencil
straight pins, scissors

METHOD:

1. ☆ Trace the pattern for the mask onto the tracing paper and then pin the tracing paper to the felt.

2. ☆ Cut around the outside edges and then the two holes for the eyes.

3. ☆ At each end of the mask cut a tiny hole with the scissors and attach a 12″ length of ribbon or string.

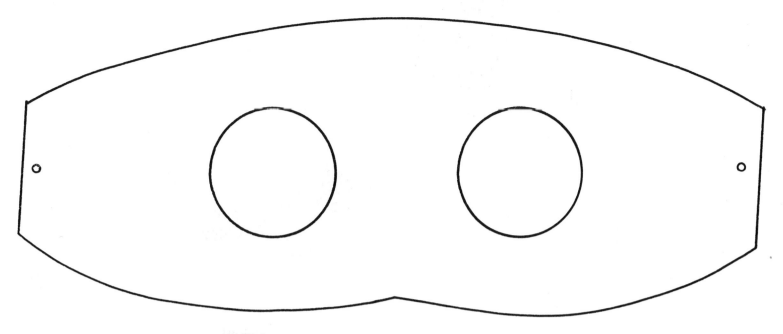

Scars Galore

With some poster paints you can quickly become a scar-faced monster. You may want to apply the Count and Countess Morbida makeup first.

MATERIALS:

red, purple and black poster paints
paintbrush
cotton balls

METHOD:

1. ☆ With a cotton ball, rub a small amount of purple paint around the area where you are going to make your scar. This will make it look like a bruise. Let it dry.

2. ☆ With either the black or red paint make a long line. Make stitches—short lines—across the long line.

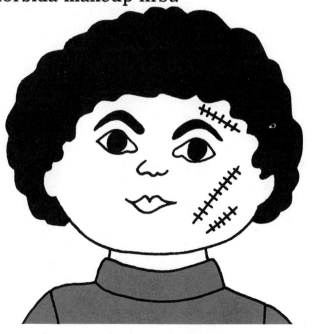

Vampire Fangs

Almost the real thing, and great fun to make and wear. You can put on the Count or Countess Morbida makeup, put on a horror hand, the cape, and the fangs for a grand costume.

MATERIALS:

white plastic bottle (that contained
    dishwashing liquid)
scissors
pencil

METHOD:

1. ☆ It is important that you wash out the plastic bottle *very* thoroughly. Use a piece that has a curve so that it can easily be held in your mouth by the upper lip.

2. ☆ Checking the illustration, draw the shape onto the plastic with a pencil. Cut it out and then put it into your mouth. Instant fangs! Make sure there are no rough spots on the plastic. Use an emery board to file any roughness away.

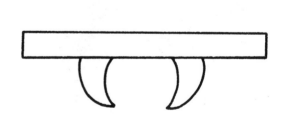

Dracula's Blood

Fun to mix up. You can apply it to yourself, or just leave it looking evil in the jar.

MATERIALS:

red, yellow and blue poster paint
1 cup corn syrup
empty jar (such as a peanut butter jar)
spoon
2 1/2″ square piece of paper
red felt tip marker
tape

METHOD:

1. ☆ Put the corn syrup into the empty jar. Add 1 teaspoon red poster paint and a few drops of yellow and blue paint. Experiment until you get a good color.

2. ☆ Stir until combined. With the red felt tip marker write "DRACULA'S BLOOD" on the paper and tape it to the jar. Presto: "real" blood!

Tricky Treat Bag

You will need a bag to carry the Halloween goodies that you collect on your rounds as you go trick or treating. Decorate a solid-colored shopping bag with these cut paper silhouettes. Designs are given for a haunted house, jack o'lantern, witch, vulture, toad, ghost and moon. Sign your bag so everyone will know you made it.

MATERIALS:

solid-color shopping bag
tracing paper
scissors, pencil
black construction paper
glue

METHOD:

1. ☆ Select the pattern you like.

2. ☆ Trace the pattern from the book and then cut out the tracing. Tape the tracing paper pattern on the black construction paper.

3. ☆ Cut out the construction paper along the pattern lines.

4. ☆ Checking the illustration, center the design on your shopping bag, and glue in place.

29

32

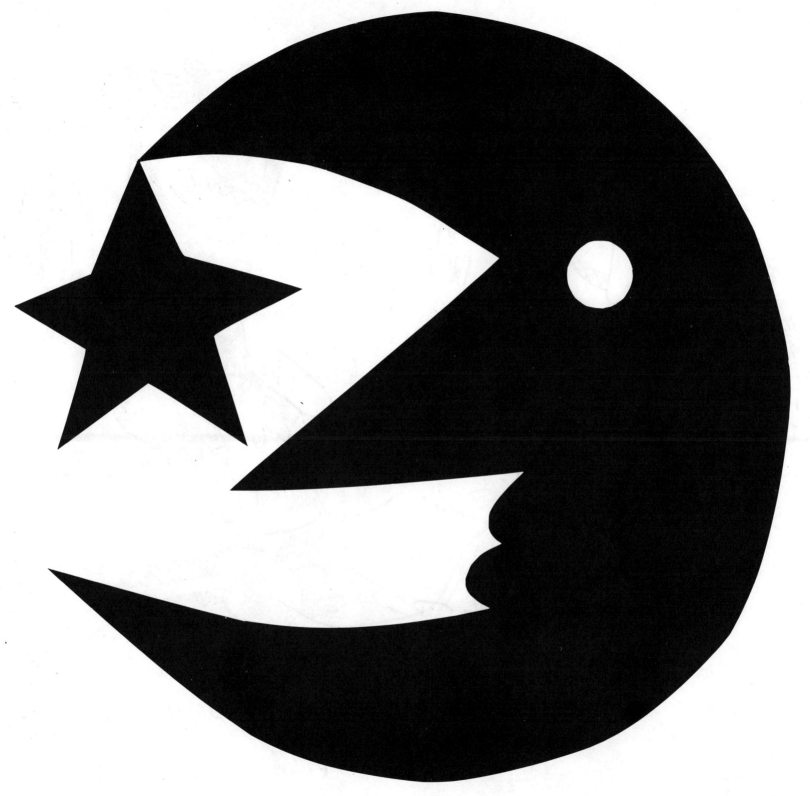

34

Parade of Monsters Stationery

Here are some monster designs to mix and match on Halloween stationery, cards or party invitations.

MATERIALS:

white paper ($8\frac{1}{2} \times 11''$)
oaktag
tracing paper, carbon paper
pencil, scissors, tape
black fine line felt tip marker
colored felt tip markers
hole punch, string

METHOD:

1. ☆ Trace the design you want on tracing paper.

2. Place a piece of carbon paper on the paper or oaktag you are using and tape it down gently. Now tape the traced design on top of the carbon paper.

3. ☆ For your stationery, use an $8\frac{1}{2} \times 11''$ piece of white paper. You can make one monster on the upper left hand corner and write around it. Or you can fill the page with monsters and just leave a small space at the bottom for a message—a short one!

For a Halloween card, fold the white paper in half and then put one or more monsters on the cover.

For the party invitation, use the oaktag and cut around the outside edge of the design. Then punch a hole at the top of the card and put a string about 8'' long through it. The reverse side of the card can be used for writing your message.

4. ☆ Draw over the design firmly with a pencil. Then remove the tracing paper and carbon paper. Now draw over the outline of the design with a fine line felt tip marker. Color in the rest of the design as you like.

Pumpkin-Face Cake

So easy—just use chocolate cake mix and save your time and energy for making icing and decorating the cake!

INGREDIENTS YOU WILL NEED:

chocolate cake mix (follow directions on the cake box for any additional ingredients for the cake)
$\frac{1}{2}$ cup orange juice
3 tablespoons sugar
1 tablespoon cornstarch
$\frac{1}{2}$ cup evaporated milk
3 egg yolks
1 teaspoon orange extract
a few drops of food coloring
M&M chocolate candies

UTENSILS YOU WILL NEED:

13″ × 9″ × 2″ pan
butter for greasing the pan
mixing bowl and spoon
measuring cups and spoons
knife to spread the icing
double boiler or two different size saucepans

DIRECTIONS:

The Cake

Follow the directions on the cake mix box; pour the cake batter into a greased 13″ × 9″ × 2″ pan. Bake as directed. Allow to cool.

The Icing

1. ☆ You will need to use a double boiler for the icing. If you do not have one, fill a small saucepan 1/4 full with cold water and put a slightly larger saucepan on top. The saucepan must be just large enough to fit halfway down the bottom pot, so that the top pot rests on water.

2. ☆ Mix together the sugar and the cornstarch in the top of the double boiler (or the large saucepan). Add the milk and continue to stir until it is smooth. Continue to cook until the mixture begins to thicken slightly.

3. ☆ Beat in the egg yolks. Add the orange juice and the orange extract. Continue to add the milk while stirring, and continue to cook until thick.

4. ☆ Add food coloring. Set aside until cool.

Decorating Your Cake:

1. ☆ To make a pumpkin face cake, follow the illustration and cut your cake into the shape of a large pumpkin, using as much of the cake as possible. The stem can be made from a scrap piece of cake and attached to the "pumpkin" with icing.

2. ☆ With a broad knife spread the icing over the rest of the cake—allow the icing to set for five minutes.

3. ☆ Create your "pumpkin's" eyes, nose, and mouth with different color M&M's—check the illustration for placement. Cover the stem with green M&M's.

4. ☆ Serve your pumpkin cake on a large platter on which you have first placed paper doilies. You may make your own platter easily by taking a heavy piece of cardboard (about the size of the pan that you baked the cake in) and covering it with tinfoil.

Sweet Licks

Caramel apples to be made in a flash and eaten right away or given to trick-or-treaters.

INGREDIENTS YOU WILL NEED:

6 small to medium size apples
1 pound caramel candies
2 tablespoons water
6 popsicle sticks (from crafts supply store)

DIRECTIONS:

1. ☆ Wash and thoroughly dry apples.

2. ☆ Heat and stir all ingredients over *very low* heat until caramels are melted and smooth.

UTENSILS YOU WILL NEED:

Medium size saucepan
Long-handled wooden spoon
Measuring spoons
Wax paper

3. ☆ Insert sticks in apples and dip into caramel. Twirl apples until completely coated.

4. ☆ Place apples on wax paper, stick end up, and refrigerate until hard—about $\frac{1}{2}$ hour.

Spicy Apple Cider

Good after a cold night's trick-or-treating!

INGREDIENTS YOU WILL NEED:

1 quart apple cider
6 cinnamon sticks or powdered cinnamon

UTENSILS YOU WILL NEED:

1 medium size saucepan

Heat cider until bubbles form around edge of saucepan. Pour into mugs or glasses and stir each with a cinnamon stick or sprinkle with a little powdered cinnamon. Cinnamon stick or glass or mug could be decorated with this pumpkin design for an extra party touch.

Bumpkin Pumpkin Butter Cookies

These cookies are easily shaped into a small pumpkin shape. The center of each can be filled with jam, a walnut, or a chocolate candy.

INGREDIENTS YOU WILL NEED:

1/4 lb. salt butter, softened.
1/4 cup sugar
1 egg yolk (Separate white from yolk by gently cracking egg open around the middle and letting white run out as you move yolk back and forth between the two halves of the shell.)
1 cup flour (heaping)
strawberry jam, or walnuts, or small chocolate candies

UTENSILS YOU WILL NEED:

large mixing bowl
beater
spatula
2 cookie sheets
measuring cups
wax paper

DIRECTIONS:

1. ☆ Set the oven at 350°—you may need an adult to help.

2. ☆ Cream the soft butter and the sugar together with a beater.

3. ☆ Stir in the egg yolk and then gradually add the flour.

4. ☆ Form into a ball. Wrap in wax paper. Refrigerate for one-half hour.

5. ☆ To make the cookies, take a little bit of the dough into your hand and roll into a small ball. Pinch the top edge slightly and draw out a small piece to make the pumpkin's stem. With your finger, make a hole in the center of each cookie and fill with jam, a walnut, or a chocolate candy.

6. ☆ Place the cookies on the cookie sheets and bake for about 20—25 minutes or until slightly browned.

41

Pumpkin Bread

Pumpkin bread is an old-fashioned American favorite. It has a gingerbread flavor and is delicious to eat when spread with either butter or cream cheese. It is especially good at Halloween.

INGREDIENTS YOU WILL NEED:

2 cups presifted flour
2 teaspoons baking powder
1/4 teaspoon baking soda
1 teaspoon salt
1 teaspoon cinnamon
1/4 teaspoon ginger
1/2 cup butter
1 cup light brown sugar, firmly packed
2 eggs
1 cup canned pumpkin
1/2 cup milk
1/2 cup seedless raisins
extra butter to grease the pan

UTENSILS YOU WILL NEED:

beater
9″ × 5″ × 3″ loaf pan
large mixing bowl
spatula
measuring cups and spoons
serving plate

DIRECTIONS:

1. ☆ Set the oven at 350°—you may need an adult to help.

2. ☆ Combine the first six ingredients and set aside.

3. ☆ Cream the butter and sugar well. Beat in the eggs, then stir in the canned pumpkin.

4. ☆ Add the dry ingredients and the milk alternately to the creamed mixture.

5. ☆ Add the raisins and then pour into a 9″ × 5″ × 3″ loaf pan that has been greased with the extra butter.

6. ☆ Bake for 50 to 60 minutes or until done. *Gently* press a fingertip on the bread —the mark you make will quickly disappear if bread is done. Or insert a toothpick in the center. There should not be any moist dough on the toothpick when you withdraw it. Allow to cool in the pan for about 15 minutes and then transfer to a serving plate.

Ghostly Lollipops

This is a clever way to disguise a lollipop and make it into a friendly ghost.

MATERIALS:

package of lollipops
white tissue paper
1/4″ orange ribbon, 8″ long for *each* lollipop.
   Multiply by number of lollipops to know
   how much ribbon you will need.
black felt tip marker
scissors

METHOD:

1. ☆ For each "ghost," cut the tissue paper into an 8″ square. Then cut the orange ribbon into an 8″ length.

2. ☆ Put the lollipop candy in the center of the tissue paper and crumple the paper around it to form the ghost's head. Tie ribbon around the part where the paper meets the stick. Make a bow.

3. ☆ Checking the illustration, draw a face onto the head of each ghost.

Jeremy Jack-O'-Lantern

Part of the magic of Halloween is the glowing jack-o'-lantern on a friendly window or doorstep. Here are four different faces to choose from when carving your pumpkin this year . . . a happy face, sad face, scary face, and a weird one! And save the pumpkin seeds for use in another project (see page 47).

MATERIALS:

pumpkin
paper towels
knife, spoon
empty tin can
candle
pencil

METHOD:

1. ☆ Wipe your pumpkin with a damp paper towel so that it is clean and shiny. Decide which face you are going to use and then draw it on your pumpkin with a pencil, checking the illustration. Be sure to leave room at the top to cut a lid in the pumpkin.

2. ☆ Remove the seeds from inside the pumpkin with a spoon. Keep the seeds in paper towels for use in another project (see page 47).

When the lid and the inside of the pumpkin have been scraped clean, you can begin to carve out the features with a knife.

3. ☆ Wash and then thoroughly dry an empty tuna fish or other small tin can. Turn this can into a candleholder by first melting the bottom of the candle slightly and then pressing it into the tin. Now place the candle in its holder inside the pumpkin, and replace

the pumpkin lid . . . your jack-o'-lantern is now ready to glow!

Note: You may need help from an adult with the knife and matches needed in this project.

Popcorn Balls

Treats that are fun to make with a few friends. These tasty morsels can also be tinted orange especially for Halloween, or made in a caramel flavor.

INGREDIENTS YOU WILL NEED:

5 quarts popped unsalted popcorn
2 1/2 cups granulated sugar
3/4 cup light corn syrup
2/3 cup butter
1/2 cup water
1/8 teaspoon cream of tartar
2 teaspoons salt
1 teaspoon vanilla
1 cup ice water
extra butter (to put on your hands)

UTENSILS YOU WILL NEED:

saucepan
small bowl (for ice water)
measuring cups and spoons
metal spoon
wax paper
plastic sandwich bags
orange ribbon

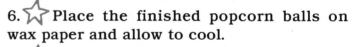

DIRECTIONS:

1. ☆ Combine the sugar, light corn syrup, water, butter, cream of tartar and salt in a saucepan and cook over low flame.

2. ☆ Keep a glass of ice water handy. Drop a little cooked syrup from a teaspoon into the ice water. When the syrup separates into brittle threads, the mixture is cooked enough.

3. ☆ Remove from heat and mix in the vanilla.

4. ☆ Carefully pour the syrup over the popcorn, trying to coat evenly. Let cool enough to handle.

5. ☆ Making sure that your hands are clean, put some butter on them. Now take some of the mixture into your hands and quickly shape into balls about the size of tennis balls.

6. ☆ Place the finished popcorn balls on wax paper and allow to cool.

7. ☆ To add an extra special touch, put each popcorn ball into a plastic bag and tie with a piece of orange ribbon.

VARIATIONS:

Orange popcorn balls: Tint the syrup with a few drops of yellow food coloring and flavor the syrup with orange extract instead of the vanilla.

Caramel popcorn balls: Use $2\frac{1}{2}$ cups of light brown sugar (firmly packed) instead of the granulated sugar, and dark corn syrup instead of the light syrup.

Pumpkin Seed Mosaic Card

This neat Halloween card is made from pumpkin seeds that were taken from your jack-o'-lantern.

MATERIALS:

pumpkin seeds from your
 jack-o'-lantern—see page 44
paper towels
8 1/2″ square of cardboard
medium size mixing bowl
pencil
glue
green, orange, and black felt tip markers

METHOD:

1. ☆ Clean the seeds and wash and dry thoroughly.

2. ☆ Using the orange felt tip marker, draw a border on the cardboard $\frac{1}{4}″$ from the outside edge.

3. ☆ With a pencil roughly draw in the outline of the pumpkin shape and its features. Check the illustration as you are drawing.

4. ☆ Beginning with the eyes, nose, and then the mouth, fill in the shapes with pumpkin seeds as they best follow your outline. The seeds don't have to follow the outline exactly to give a pleasing mosaic effect, so don't worry if every space isn't filled.

5. ☆ Use the black marker to darken the outlines around the eyes, nose, and mouth, so that they will stand out from the pumpkin face.

6. ☆ Now completely fill in the pumpkin with the pumpkin seeds, then color over the seeds with orange marker. Next fill in the stem with pumpkin seeds and color them with green marker.

7. ☆ Finish your card by writing your Halloween message and signing your name on the bottom.

47

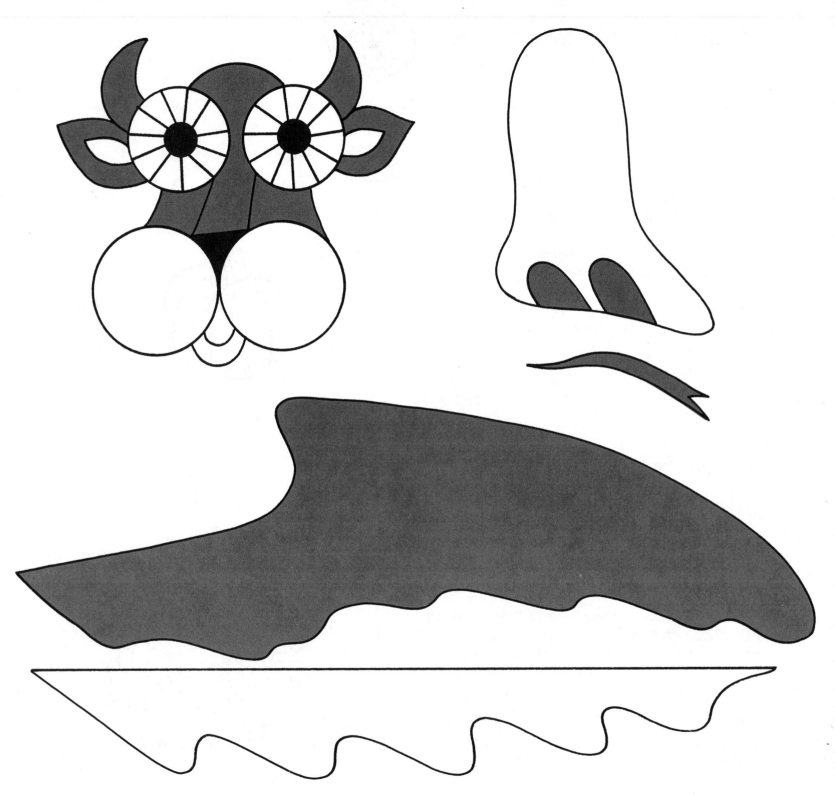

Marcel the Monster

An egg carton becomes a winged monster ready to decorate your room for Halloween. If a group of you work together there could be a parade of horrible creatures!

MATERIALS:

1 empty egg carton
white and green oaktag
tracing paper
scrap of red felt
black felt tip marker
pencil, glue
scissors

METHOD:

1. ☆ Make a pattern for the monster's head, wing, leg, tail, and tongue by tracing the designs given.

2. ☆ Place the patterns on the oaktag and trace around the outlines with a pencil. The head should be made from the white oaktag and the tongue from the red felt. Everything else should be made from the green oaktag. Be sure to make two wings and four legs.

3. ☆ Checking the illustration, draw in the monster's features with a black felt tip marker. Use the marker to color in his toenails as well.

4. ☆ Place the egg carton upside down, as shown, and glue shut.

5. ☆ Glue the head, wings, legs, and long tongue in place, as shown. Make sure the wings are each going in the right direction.

Virgil the Vampire Pop-Up Card

A vampire pops up at you from the inside fold of this Halloween card . . . a fun fright for your favorite friends!

MATERIALS:

10″ × 16″ piece of white paper
tracing paper
carbon paper
pencil, scissors
tape
black, fine line felt tip marker
red, black, grey felt tip markers

METHOD:

1. ☆ Trace the design for the card on tracing paper.

2. ☆ Fold the 10″ × 16″ paper in half along the 10″ side.

3. ☆ Place a piece of carbon paper on the folded paper—fold should be at the bottom. Tape the carbon paper down gently. Now tape the traced design on top of the carbon paper—check the illustration for placement.

4. ☆ Draw over the design firmly with a pencil. Then remove the tracing paper and carbon paper. Now draw over the outline of the design with a fine line felt tip marker.

5. ☆ Fold the paper along the 16″ side.

6. ☆ To make the fold that will allow the vampire to pop up when the card is opened, first measure down 5″ from the center fold of the inside of the card (point A). Then measure 1¼″ in from each side and 2″ down on each side (points B and C). Follow the illustration

as you go along. With a pencil draw a line from point A to point B and from point A to point C. Fold the paper along these lines. Erase the pencil lines.

7. ☆ Checking the illustration, cut away the upper part of the card along the vampire's cape and hands.

8. ☆ Color in the vampire's eyes, nails, mouth and cape with red marker. Color his eyebrows and hair with black marker and his suit grey.

9. ☆ Fold the card so that the vampire is on the inside and the front is blank. Write "OPEN ME" on the front in large letters, and on the inside write "Have a fang-tastic Halloween!"

step ①

step ②

10"

fold →

16"

step ③

step ⑤

fold

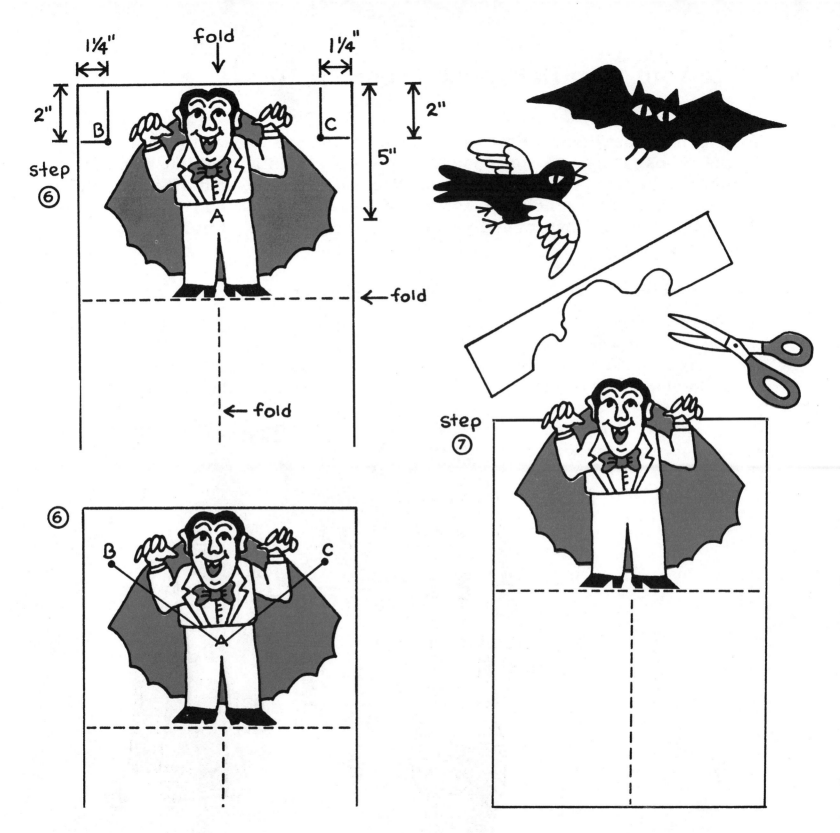

1¼"   fold   1¼"

2"

step
⑥

B   C

5"

2"

A

← fold

← fold

⑥

B   C

A

step
⑦

53

Write Your Own Halloween Poem

You can be a poet! Here are two original poems and some ideas to inspire you. On the opposite page are some poems that were written a long time ago. They should also help to put you in the mood. Read all the poems and the words and phrases. Then take a pencil and write down your own ideas and rhymes. Think about all the things that remind you of Halloween and what fun it is to go out "trick or treating."

I Like Halloween

I do like Halloween
because of all the things that can't be seen,
ghosts and bats that fly in the night,
waiting for the moon's first light.

I go out and play all day,
but when the sun goes down
ghoulish monsters run around—
so it's straight inside for me
to warm friends and company!

Witch of Wentworth

The wicked witch of Wentworth Wood
was always up to no good.
She did whatever she could
to create mischief in the woods.

SOME OLD POEMS

Jerry Jones

Six feet beneath
This funeral wreath
Is laid upon the shelf
One Jerry Jones,
Who dealt in bones,
And now he's bones himself.

Author Unknown

A Skeleton Once in Khartoum

A skeleton once in Khartoum
Asked a spirit up into his room;
    They spent the whole night
    In the eeriest fight
As to which should be frightened of whom.

Author Unknown

Ghoulies and Beasties

From Ghoulies and Ghosties,
And long-leggity Beasties,
And all things that go bump
    in the night,
Good Lord deliver us.

Old Cornish Litany

In Memory of Anna Hopewell

Here lies the body of Anna
Done to death by a banana
It wasn't the fruit that laid her low
But the skin of the thing that made her go.

Author Unknown

The Kilkenny Cats

There wanst was two cats at Kilkenny,
Each thought there was one cat too many,
  So they quarrel'd and fit,
  They scratch'd and they bit,
  Till, excepting their nails,
  And the tips of their tails,
Instead of two cats, there warnt any.

Author Unknown

WORDS AND PHRASES TO INSPIRE YOUR POEMS

haunted houses
invisible spirits
ghosts
demons and devils
monsters and witches
vampire bats
zombie
full moon
toads
devils
ghastly moans
strange voices
October night
autumn moon
graveyard antics
black cats
owls
flying witches
vultures
pumpkins
snakes
shadows
chilling, thrilling
spooky
shiver and quake
evil creatures of the night
starry night
rustling leaves
musty smells
glowing jack-o'-lanterns

Benton the Black Cat

You can hang Benton up as a party decoration or make several of him to give as special Halloween treats.

MATERIALS:

tracing paper
chalk (white), scissors
needle, straight pins
black thread
2 squares of black felt
scraps of red and white felt
polyester batting
glue

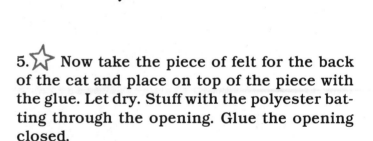

METHOD:

1. ☆ Make a pattern for the cat by tracing the design given.

2. ☆ Put one piece of black felt on top of the other and pin together. Place the pattern on top of the felt and trace around the outline with a piece of chalk. Cut on the chalked line.

3. ☆ To make the cat's features cut the whiskers from the white felt and two small circles for eyes. Cut a tongue from the red felt. Checking the illustration, glue the features in place.

4. ☆ Take the piece of felt with the features on it and turn it over to the reverse side. Carefully spread a small amount of glue all along the outside edge, leaving the bottom (the cat's stomach) free of glue.

5. ☆ Now take the piece of felt for the back of the cat and place on top of the piece with the glue. Let dry. Stuff with the polyester batting through the opening. Glue the opening closed.

6. ☆ Thread the needle with black thread and sew through the cat to make a hanger, as shown. Now you can hang Benton the Black Cat up in your room!

Orson the Needlepoint Owl

This is a quickie needlepoint project. The background is colored with marker so all you really have to stitch is the owl himself, the moon, and some super-quick stars in the sky.

MATERIALS:

single mesh needlepoint canvas, 8½″ square
4-ply tapestry yarn in black, yellow, tan, white
   and brown
blunt tapestry needle (size 18 with large eye)
blue felt tip marker
pencil, ruler
tape, scissors
tracing paper, carbon paper
cardboard, 10″ square
strip of brightly colored fabric, 4″ × 40″ or 12″
   square

METHOD:

The stitches

To make this owl in needlepoint you will be using three stitches: half-cross, satin, and star. If you follow the illustrations and practice the stitches a few times on a scrap of canvas you will quickly learn them.

Half-cross Stitch

This is the basic stitch in needlepoint and is used to cover a single intersection (crossing point) of the canvas threads. You work the halfcross stitch from the bottom left part of the intersection putting the yarn into the section above on the diagonal—the upper right. This stitch is always done on the slant, and all stitches must slant in the same direction. Keep repeating this until the area that is to be completed is filled up.

Satin Stitch

This stitch is used to cover large areas of canvas. Work the satin stitch over 4 or 6 threads of the canvas to form steps, as shown. This stitch is worked up and down.

Star Stitch ✳ ✳ ✳

Make a cross stitch by first making a half-cross stitch from lower right to upper left, and then crossing it with another half-cross stitch going the opposite way, from lower left to upper right. Now make a straight cross stitch over this, from left to right and then from top to bottom.

Preparing the canvas

1. ☆ Put tape all around the edges of the 8½″ square of needlepoint canvas. This will prevent the edges from ravelling.

2. ☆ Trace the owl design using the tracing paper. Place a piece of carbon paper on top of the canvas and tape it down. Now tape the traced owl on top of the carbon paper, centering the owl on the canvas. Draw over the design firmly with a pencil, then remove the carbon and tracing paper from the canvas.

3. ☆ Color in the background sky with blue felt tip marker.

The yarn

It is easiest to work with a piece of yarn about 18″ long when doing needlepoint (except for the star stitch, for which you should use 25″). Knot one end of the yarn and thread the other end through the needle. Put the needle through the canvas with one hand and with the other hand hold the knot. You will have to hold the knot down for a few stitches so that the yarn won't slip through the canvas. To end a thread when it gets short, go through 2 or 3 stitches on the wrong side of the canvas. This will prevent the stitches that you have made from becoming undone.

Needlepointing the owl

1. ☆ To needlepoint the owl check the illustration to see which stitches are to be used where. Start with the owl's eyes, which should be half-cross stitched. The circle around the eyes and the beak are to be done in the satin stitch. The rest of the head and the claws should be half-cross stitched. The owl's wings, chest, and the branch that he is perched on are to be done in the satin stitch.

2. ☆ The owl's eyes should be done with black yarn. The circles around his eyes, his claws, and the moon should be done with yellow yarn. The owl's beak, wings, and the branch should be done with brown yarn. His head and chest should be done with tan yarn.

3. ☆ Now make stars in the sky with the white yarn using the star stitch.

Framing your needlepoint

To make the frame for your needlepoint you can use the 10″ square of cardboard. Cut an 8″ square from the center of the cardboard to make a "window" to show your needlepoint. You may wish to cover the cardboard frame with brightly colored fabric, which can be wrapped around the frame and pasted or stapled to the back. The frame should be centered over the needlepoint, which can be taped in place from the back.

Half-cross Stitch

Satin Stitch

Star Stitch

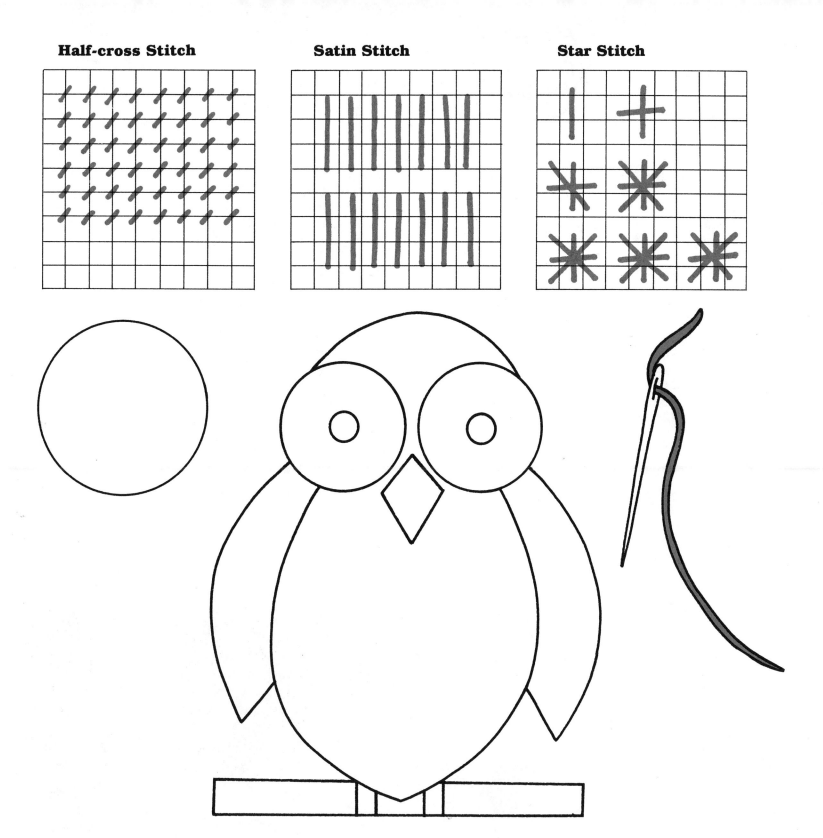

Index